AF700446

WHAT CLIENTS HAVE TO SAY

Plain and simple, Profit First makes the most sense of any accounting system I have ever used. It is based on real data and real attainable goals. Barb is kind and caring and I thoroughly enjoyed working with her. I will never go back to my "old" ways. Her program changed the way I manage my practice for the rest of my career.

Dr. Abby Neville; Neville Dental Care, PA

Working with Barb has been a tremendous eye opener about how to run the financial aspect of a dental practice. However, she does so much more. She can help with almost any area of one's practice. In addition, Barb is a great "dental therapist" who has an unusual ability to help calm me down about the stressors and challenges of running a dental practice. The ABSOLUTE best money I ever invested in my dental practice.

Dr. Matt Galfund; Galfund Family Dentistry, NJ

I had the pleasure of working with Barbara for six months in our journey to incorporate Profit First into my practice. Understanding our financials and the P&L was never easy for me. After reading both *Profit First* and *Profit First for Dentists,* I felt this could be the solution I was looking for. After reviewing our numbers and creating a budget based on previous months of income and expenses, Barbara was able to coach me through the process of allocating a percentage of our revenue into 4 categories: Profit, Owners Compensation, Taxes and Operational Expenses. Each week I would transfer the percentage of funds to the appropriate account to allow us to easily see where we stood financially. We spent many coaching calls over the months evaluating the accuracy and explaining what to look for in order to make changes in the future for additional profits and expenses for growth. She helped me realize that Profit First is a mindset. Always pay the Profit First, which became much easier once I realized that the monies were allocated to allow that to happen. Barbara, I need to say thank you for all your support and guidance through the process. I could not have done it without you.

Dr. David Faust; Bucks County Smiles, PA

We approached Barb to help us with the profit first concept after we read her book and realized this would help us to optimize our office finances so that we could be rewarded for the hard work that we put in daily. From the first meeting with Barb, she had helpful tips and information which helped us from day one. I think the biggest thing that we have learned is that you need to track information and data to gather information to help guide you in your decision-making. If you do not track your data, you do not know if you're performing well or not. Barb not only helped us with looking at our data from different angles, but she also assisted us personally in making decisions to help improve our overall service at JVR Dental. April was a great support in terms of Canadian tax resources to make sure we were doing everything above board when it came to business taxes.

Both Barb and April are amazing people to work with and I can almost guarantee that they will improve your financial position in your clinic when they get involved.

Mauritz Lundt; Office Manager, Dr. Leana Lundt, JVR Dental, BC Canada

PROFIT FIRST FOR DENTISTS GUIDEBOOK

PROFIT FIRST FOR DENTISTS GUIDEBOOK

A WORKBOOK TO HELP YOU GET THE MOST FROM *PROFIT FIRST FOR DENTISTS*

BARBARA STACKHOUSE

RDH, M.Ed.
Mastery Profit First Professional
Author of *Profit First for Dentists*

More to Life.Dental, Goodlettsville, Tennessee, 37072, USA

© 2024 by Union Hill Press
Barbara Stackhouse, RDH, M.Ed.

All rights reserved. No part of this publication may be reproduced, distributed, or transmitted in any form or by any means, including photocopying, recording, or other electronic or mechanical methods, without the prior written permission of the publisher—except in the case of brief quotations embodied in critical reviews and certain other noncommercial uses permitted by copyright.
Inquiries regarding permission for use of the material contained in this book should be addressed via email to More to Life.Dental: Barb@Moreto-Life.Dental

ISBN: 978-1-7359078-3-3

Disclaimer:
The information contained within this book is for informational purposes only. It should not be considered financial, legal, or tax advice. You should consult with your own bookkeeper, CPA, attorney, or tax professional to make decisions for your own personal and professional needs.

Page design & typesetting by Chinook Design, Inc. (chinooktype.com)

CONTENTS

Introduction

After 20 years of coaching and consulting in the Dental Practice Management space with the last 6 of those years owning my own business, I find dentists still grappling with the same issues when it comes to the business side of the practice.

I am so very grateful to my dentist client, Dr. Steven Schlentz, who introduced me to the Profit First book by Mike Michalowicz. When I read Mike's book, I knew this would be a game changer for my clients. But I also knew Mike didn't know dentistry.

Lumping dentistry into the mix of all other professions doesn't work when it comes to the percentage of overhead. I sometimes hear patients say, "Dentistry is expensive" and I always respond, "Yes, it is." Dentistry is an expensive profession. The cost of a dental education continues to rise. The cost of owning a practice is also on the rise. And once you own a practice, the expenses seem never ending.

So how does a dentist manage all the things? Great question! I believe once you get the finances under control, it's easier to manage everything else. And, it's possible to slow down and enjoy the journey instead of always feeling chained to the chair producing more and more dentistry trying to get ahead.

At the time of my writing this introduction, it was 10 weeks ago when my life changed. I was on vacation enjoying a beautiful day with my husband and dear friends. I was totally unaware of a serious problem brewing in my body. Just 5 days prior, I had started a new medication. Little did I know I was having a serious reaction.

I don't remember anything about what happened next. I passed out and fell face first onto a concrete floor. When I came to, I remember asking what happened and realized I had a front tooth missing. Number 9 was completely avulsed and all of my front teeth were fractured and broken. It truly was a hygienist's nightmare.

My tooth was found. I put it back in. Miraculously, within 30 minutes I was sitting in a dental chair and a dentist and oral surgeon worked for 2 hours putting my mouth back together. The oral surgeon showed me the x-ray with my palate bone broken in 2 places where #9 had avulsed. We then traveled back home to Nashville where my dentist referred me to an endodontist.

Unfortunately, my experience at this endodontist did not go well. I waited for over an hour to be seen. The doctor saw me for about 10 minutes, prescribed 4 root canals, and sent me to the front to schedule. I decided pretty quickly, this was not the office for me.

I reached out to my general dentist, and let her know I needed a referral to a different endodontist and I had decided I would prefer to see a biologic endodontist. My dentist reached out to her biologic dentistry community. They recommended a biologic endodontist in Texas. I live in Tennessee so this meant I would need to travel for my care.

A few weeks later, I was on a flight to Texas to see the biologic endodontist. My experience at this office was amazing. They were ready for me when I arrived. I was the only patient scheduled for the entire morning. The doctor saw me right away and she took her time in reviewing the CBCT x-ray and did a very comprehensive examination. Turns out I needed 7 root canals. I had 2 slight fractures in my chin in addition to the 2 fractures in my palate.

I tell you this story because it illustrates exactly what I teach to dentists. When finances are under control and you are not worrying about money, you can slow down and focus more on your patients. You can spend more time with each patient and give them your best. I truly believe that your patients want you to be profitable. They want the best you have to offer.

The biologic endodontist I saw had a small office. The equipment was clean and worked great, but it was clearly not new. There were worn spots and scratches. I didn't go to her for her equipment. I chose her because she came highly recommended, and she had a biologic approach. She was exactly what I was looking for. She took her time. She was not rushed. She put all of her focus on me and my care.

I'm happy to say I'm doing well, and I have completed the 7 root canals. I will have restorative work completed in due time.

My hope is that my story will inspire you to take a look at your own practice. Do you have the time to spend with patients and give them your best. Could you schedule just one patient for an entire morning? Or maybe even the entire day? What would that even look like?

Do you have your finances organized with systems in place, so you don't have to worry?

Do you know where you stand with regards to your money?

Do you pay the bills with ease?

Are you constantly worrying about enough money in the account for payroll?

What is your stress level on a scale of 1 to 10; 10 being the highest level of stress possible?

If you've read this far, and know you need some help, I invite you to dive deep into my Profit First for Dentists book and keep this guidebook handy so you can do the work as you read. And yes, please do the work. It's the only way to make the shift into a new financially prosperous life.

Stay committed. Find an accountability partner. Press on even in the face of adversity. Don't let anyone tell you it can't be done.

You alone are the owner of your choices and your destiny. What will you choose?

Barb Stackhouse RDH, M.Ed.

1

The Business of Owning a Dental Practice

1

IT'S TIME TO DO SOME WRITING

In case this is new to you, it's called journaling. I encourage you to write. Write what comes to your mind. Write even when it doesn't make sense. Write when you feel resistance. Write in the morning. Write at night. Write.

Okay, you get the idea. Let's get serious here. I am here to tell you if you do the work, you will get results. You decide what results you want. Then, do the work and go after the results.

Read Chapter One in the book, *Profit First for Dentists.* Then come back here to this guidebook and use the journal prompts to complete your writing exercises. Take your time. There is no rush.

Yes, it's important to complete the journaling exercises. That's why they are included here for you. Duh! In all seriousness, our thoughts become our reality. Get your thoughts out of you and on to paper. Read them again. Is there anything you want to change about your thoughts? Your future?

Journaling gives you the chance to connect with yourself and make the choices necessary to propel you forward into your dreams. Remember everything is first created within (in your thoughts and dreams) and then when you make the choice to turn it into reality, it is created again by your actions.

Let's get started. Happy journaling!

JOURNAL

What is your dental story?
How did you get into dentistry? What brought you to where you are today? Write it out completely.

QUESTIONS

Do you have business debt? ______________________

How much? ______________________

When will it be paid off? ______________________

What is it for?

JOURNAL

What is your biggest worry in your practice? Why does this worry you?

QUESTIONS

How much do you have saved for retirement (when you exit the practice)? ____________________

How much do you need to have saved when you exit the practice? ____________________
(If you don't know, it's time to find a great financial advisor.)
Is there a gap? What is the dollar amount of the gap? ____________________

At what age will you exit the practice? ____________________

JOURNAL

What is the story you tell yourself about your business? Is the story in your head positive or negative? Do you want to change your story? Why or Why not?

JOURNAL

Is there chatter going on in your mind all day long? What is the chatter telling you? Is this true?

JOURNAL

When you think about Profitability and how it is associated with your business; What does Profit mean to you? Can you define Gross Profit and Net Profit?

ACTION STEP

Complete the Dental Practice Profit Score!
Go to **www.profitfirstdentist.com/profitscore**

What is your score?

Email me and tell me your score and what you plan to do next. **barb@barbstackhouse.com**

Continue to read each chapter in *Profit First for Dentists* and then come back to the corresponding *Guidebook* chapter and complete the exercises.

2

The Core Principles of Profit First for Dentists

2

Let's get clear on the 4 Core Principles of Profit First for Dentists and how these principles can help you transform the financial picture of your dental practice.

1. **Small Plates Principle**
2. **Sequence Matters**
3. **Remove Temptation**
4. **Enforce a Rhythm**

PROFIT FIRST CORE PRINCIPLES

The Profit First principles are rooted in behavioral science. When you work with your natural human behaviors and not against them, your success rate increases. Make sense?

1. **Small Plates Principle:** To explain this principle, we're going to explore Parkinson's Law: The demand for something expands to match its supply. We are going to explain this concept with dinner plates! Smaller plates hold less food; therefore, you eat less. Large plates hold more, leading to overeating. Who hasn't gone to a family reunion potluck and filled their plate so full they are miserable after eating?

   We do the same thing with time. When you're working on a project and you have a month to get it done, most would probably take the entire month to complete it but when you only have a few days, you somehow make it happen.

The best example of Parkinson's Law is toothpaste! When the tube is brand-new and full of toothpaste, most people squirt out a big long ribbon of paste to cover the brush. There's plenty available. But when the tube is nearly empty, we start twisting, rolling, and squeezing the tube, hoping to get any amount of toothpaste on the brush. When that small drop the size of half a pea lands on the bristles of the brush, we're celebrating inside like we've just won a trophy.

The lesson here is to notice how our behavior changes, based on what is available. What better lesson than 2020, the year of the pandemic that shut down dentistry as we know it for a few months. All of a sudden, there was less money coming in, so you instinctively began to cut costs. This happened before there was any word of a PPP loan or an Economic Injury Disaster Loan (EIDL), and they were temporary fixes anyway. When you have less, you immediately become frugal. But you also begin to get innovative and figure out new or better ways of doing things. This is a good thing—not the pandemic, but you getting frugal and innovative.

If we can all do this during a pandemic, why not make it a part of business as usual? When you have less money in your bank account, you'll get frugal and innovative. Bottom line is, you'll spend less. More on exactly how to do this in a bit.

2. **Sequence Matters:** The Primacy Effect principle helps us understand the importance of sequence and why it matters. We have a cognitive bias toward information presented first rather than later. We hold that same bias for items in the first position on a list. If you're a list maker,

you'll understand. The things at the top of the list get done first.

This is good news for implementing Profit First! Sequence does matter when it comes to your money. By changing the formula to **SALES – PROFIT = EXPENSES**, we place profit before expenses. Seriously, it's that simple! Remember, the old way using GAAP (Generally Accepted Accounting Principles), was **SALES – EXPENSES = PROFIT**. This has caused entrepreneurs to place expenses before profit. The reality is, we're always waiting for the leftovers and wondering if there will be any profit left. This is not a good plan to operate on. It's actually exhausting. If you feel like you're always grinding it out at the chair, producing and collecting more only to find your income stagnating at the same level, you know what I'm talking about.

It's time to flip the equation. Make profit the primary objective.

SALES - PROFIT = EXPENSES.

QUESTION

Are you in? Check one:

☐ Yes, I'm all in

☐ Yes, I'm interested but need to find out more (keep reading)

☐ Yes, but I feel I'm not ready (keep reading, you don't have to be ready)

☐ No, I'm not really resonating with this idea (you can still keep reading)

---

3. **Remove Temptation:** Not keeping junk food in the house makes it less convenient to get, therefore we aren't tempted to eat it. The same is true with our money. Out of sight, out of mind is the new mantra. This means we move our profit and tax into an account we don't have immediate access to. A lack of immediate access removes the temptation and we start making do with what we have for expenses.

   This is the fun part! Remember the formula **SALES** (produce and collect) minus **PROFIT** (set aside, no temptation) equals **EXPENSES** (frugal and innovative). You follow this formula and then this amazing thing happens, and with the most perfect timing: the **Profit** account releases some money to you, the owner. Bonus time, baby!! This is what your business is meant to do from the beginning, and now, with Profit First, it's a reality.

4. **Enforce a Rhythm:** We learned that bingeing and crashing on food is not in the best interest of our health, and the same is true for our money. Instead of playing catch-up or going into panic mode when all the bills are due, establish a weekly rhythm and flow to the cash coming in and going out of the business. Creating consistent cash flow week in and week out removes the panic button and replaces it with peace of mind.

   No longer will you need to read a cash flow or profit and loss (P&L) statement to know where you stand—and if we're being honest here, you don't do that anyway. Understanding cash flow will be as easy as opening your bank accounts and checking the balances (which is what we already do). This whole process is created using simple bank balance accounting. Profit First gives you the process and the measuring tool to make it happen.

QUESTIONS

Are you the type of person who will follow the strategy exactly, to ensure you get the best results? (circle one)

YES NO

Or are you already thinking about how this could work but you'll modify it slightly? (circle one)

YES NO

If you responded yes to the second question, explain why here:

It's time to make some commitments to yourself. Are you willing to open additional bank accounts to get started? (circle one)

YES NO

JOURNAL

What is the resistance you feel when you think about actually using the Profit First method?

QUESTION

Are you worried about your bookkeeper or accountant resisting the plan? (circle one)

YES NO

If you responded yes, Why do you feel this way?

QUESTIONS

Are you willing to have a conversation with your bookkeeper and/or CPA about implementing Profit First in your practice? (circle one)

YES NO

If you responded yes, when will you do it?

____

____

____

If you responded no, why not?

____

____

____

____

____

____

____

____

____

As you prepare to speak with your bookkeeper and/or accountant, here are some questions to consider.

GETTING YOUR ACCOUNTANT ON BOARD

Now is the time to talk to your accountant and get them on board with Profit First. Profit First will change nothing about how they conduct their accounting practices, but it will change everything about how you learn to have cash flow.

5 Critical Questions for a Profit Ready Dental Practice Accountant

1. Of your existing clients, how many post consistent quarterly profit?
2. Do you have a bank-based management tool?
3. How many Profit First rollouts have you completed for dentists?
4. Do you understand the unique challenges facing dental practice owners and utilize a proper Chart of Accounts for Dentists?
5. How many of the clients you serve are dentists?

JOURNAL

If you're not comfortable asking these questions, why not? What is your resistance?

JOURNAL

What are some questions that come up for you that you'd like to ask of your accountant?

3

Using Bank Accounts to Your Advantage

3

I am not here to convince you to start implementing the Profit First for Dentists method, although I will tell you many dentists are using the method with great success. I implement it in my own business with great success. It is a game changer for me. This is not about manipulating numbers to make the books look better. It's about a solid method that you connect with and helps you make something complex seem simple.

Before I jump to further explanation of the Profit First for Dentists method, I want to ask you some questions. Please be honest with yourself. These questions are for your own reflection. Take the time now to journal your answers and get really clear with yourself about your beliefs.

JOURNAL

When you want to make a purchase for your business that will require some significant cash (more than what is planned for in your monthly expenses), how do you determine if you have the money to spend?

____

____

____

____

____

____

____

____

____

QUESTION

Did your answer to the last question include looking at your account balance in your online banking? (circle one)

YES NO

If you answered YES, you are in the majority of most human beings living in North America. It truly is our natural human behavior around money to use bank account balances as a way to gauge how much cash is available on any given day.

Is this the best option available? Maybe, but probably not. When you are using one account for all transactions, it's extremely difficult to know exactly what is available for what purpose. It's likely that some of the money sitting in your main checking account is already spent. Perhaps there are taxes due or bills coming up that this money needs to be reserved for. Without a plan for the accounting of these items, it's a best guess scenario.

Too many times the money is used and then a few months later, a financial crunch is felt in the business.

QUESTIONS

Have you ever felt a financial crunch after you made a significant purchase? (circle one)

YES NO

What did you do to overcome it?

Having money and not having money both produce an emotional response. Money beliefs begin when we are young, and they are carried with us throughout our life. Sometimes our beliefs help us and sometimes they hinder our ability to experience the success we so deserve.

JOURNAL

What is your first memory of money?

How did this first experience with money impact your beliefs?

Do any of those old beliefs show up today?
What do you believe about money now as an adult?

Dig deep and explore if you are holding on to a belief that may be keeping you from the success level you desire. What do you desire?

Armed with the knowledge that most of us routinely check our bank balance when we want to make a purchase, I ask you to consider a system that takes advantage of this behavior.

It's been proven that when there is less money in the bank account, we automatically get resourceful and spend less. This is Parkinson's Law. I encourage you to go back to my book to learn more about this concept. For now, just know that less money in the account equals less spending and likewise more money in the bank account typically equals more spending.

It would make sense then to have multiple bank accounts where the money could be divided up with each account for a specific purpose. This would ensure there would be less money in each account (rather than all of it in one account) and lead to less spending.

To fully implement Profit First for Dentists, I recommend having five core bank accounts. They are as follows: **Income** account, **Profit** account, **Owner's Compensation** account, **Tax** account, and **Operating Expenses** account.

Here is a checklist to take with you to the bank when you open your accounts.

- ☐ Keep your current business checking account as your **Income** account. All the money will flow into this account. At the end of each week, money will be allocated by percentage from this account to the other four accounts.
- ☐ Open a savings account and name it **Profit**.
- ☐ Open a checking account and name it **Owner's Compensation**.
- ☐ Open a savings account and name it **Tax**.
- ☐ Open a business checking account and name it **Operating Expenses**.

Of course this is only a suggestion, you might decide you want your **Tax** account to be a checking account. That is totally fine. I'm sharing with you what most dentists I work with have done.

If you're not ready to go "all in" with Profit First for Dentists, then do one thing: open a savings account and Name it **Profit**! Start allocating and transferring 1% of all collections into this account. I promise you will be glad you did!

4

Sequence and Timing Matter

4

The Law of Primacy tells us that the things at the top of our to do checklist will likely be the things that get done. We tend to put the important things at the top of the list because we want to finish them and check them off.

Likewise, if we put Profit First in our sequence of allocations and transfers, it will likely get done.

JOURNAL

How would it feel if you put aside your profit first and the balance began to increase to a significant amount?

QUESTIONS

What would be a significant amount for you? (Yes, I want you to actually write down an amount.) ______________________

If you allocated and transferred 5% of your total collections each month, how long would it take to reach your significant amount? ______________________

JOURNAL

Now, how does that amount and time frame make you feel?

Once you try out Profit First with just one account, the **Profit** account, you're well on your way to the habit of allocations and transfers. That's correct, it's a habit. We all have money habits and now you're building muscle for a new healthy money habit.

When you are feeling successful with this one account, it's time to start thinking about the remaining three accounts. They are: **Owner's Compensation**, **Tax**, and **Operating Expenses**. If you haven't opened these accounts already, now is the time to take action. Go back to Chapter Three, go to your bank, and open the accounts. Ready, set, GO!

I sometimes hear resistance to Profit First because it may feel like you are putting money before the patients. I challenge that thinking because if you don't put your money mindset and habits first, you will always be chasing after it. It may then consume your time so much so that you are not 100% focused on your patients and your dentistry. Take care of the money systems now so you can put it behind you and then practice dentistry with the freedom of knowing you don't have to worry about finances.

JOURNAL

Using your current system, how do you evaluate the financial performance of your dental practice business? Write out* exactly *what reports you use and where you find the information you need to understand the finances of your business.

QUESTION

How often do you* actually *do this? ______________________

Your dental practice naturally has money flowing into it almost daily. It will also have money flowing out of it on a regular basis. It's always the goal to have more flowing in than you do going out.

Payroll is a regular expense you can count on. You know exactly when you need to have the money for it. The same is true for rent and other fixed expenses.

QUESTIONS

What about the variable expenses? Do you plan for when you will order supplies and when you will pay for them?

YES NO

Do you have a budget for your supplies?

YES NO

And do you have a plan to stay within the budget?

YES NO

With Profit First, it's best to establish a rhythm to the process. I recommend a weekly interval. Every day the **Income** account grows and then, once a week, you move money from the **Income** account to the other four bank accounts. This is done by percentage and then transferred to the appropriate account. More on the exact percentages later.

The majority of my clients do the allocations and transfers on Monday. This gives time for all deposits from the week prior to show up in the **Income** account.

QUESTION

What day of the week will work best for you to do your allocations and transfers? ______________________

Remember, profit is not an event. It's the process of weekly deposits into the **Profit** account so the balance is built up over time. It takes a weekly rhythm to make it happen.

Decide what day of the week you will pay bills. Block out time to make it happen.

Here's a diagram to help you visualize the Profit First process:

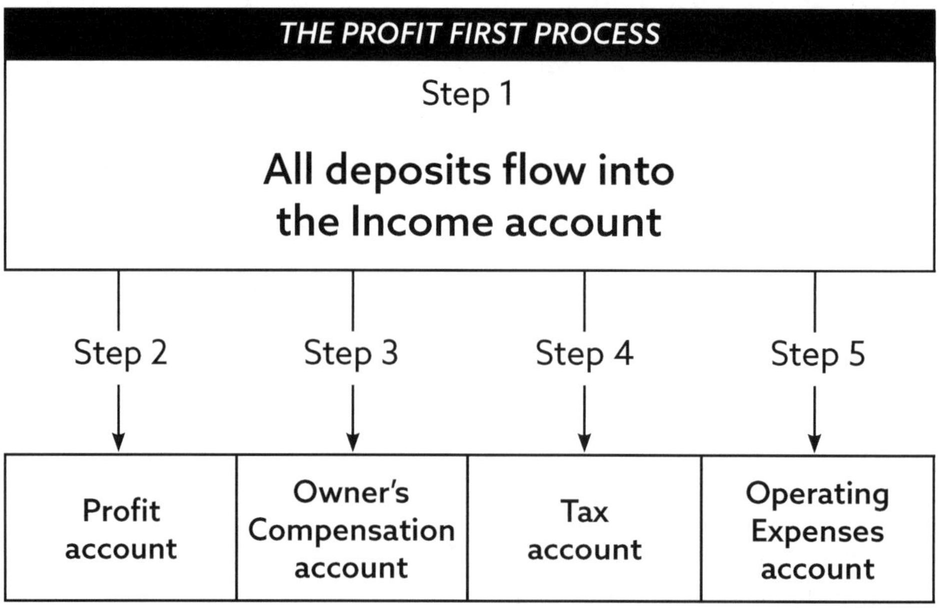

Once a week, allocate by percentage to these additional accounts in the order shown.

JOURNAL

What is your own personal motivation to implement Profit First for Dentists in your dental practice business?

Write out your motivational statement and post it somewhere you will see it daily. This will remind you often of the why behind your actions.

5

Remove Temptation

5

The temptation to spend money is real! When you are spending money from a loan or a credit card, it's easier to make the decision to spend. When you remove money from a savings account to make a purchase, there is much more thought that goes into the decision.

Let's imagine you want to equip a vacant op with a dental chair and a delivery system. You are fine with getting a refurbished chair that matches the color of what you currently have in your other ops. The total is going to be $22,000.

If you currently do not have the extra $22,000 to make this purchase, you have a choice to make. Will you put it on a credit card and pay it off over time? Or maybe you have a line of credit that you can use to make the purchase, but again, you'll be paying it off over time. Better yet, you decide to save the money and pay cash for the purchase once you have enough. If you saved $3000 per month, it would take 7.3 months to have the total saved. That's not very long to wait, and you will not have to pay interest!

But you say, "that chair is going to pay for itself and the interest with all the profit I will make by using it!" Maybe? But do you know for sure? Have you run the numbers, and do you know your true overhead including the additional loan payment?

JOURNAL

Have you ever made a rush decision on making a significant purchase for your practice where you used credit to pay for it, and how did you feel afterward when the payments began?

Have you ever saved the money up front for a significant purchase for your practice, and if so, how did you feel when making the purchase?

If you are tempted to make purchases quickly using credit, I urge you to take a step back and re-evaluate your money mindset. It may be likely that you would also steal from your **Profit** or **Tax** account to fund the **Operating Expenses** account if the funds were low. I challenge you to first consider why the funds might be low. Is there a spending problem? Was there a bad month with low collections? Try to discover the real reason first.

KICK TEMPTATION TO THE CURB!

Because Profit First is a behavioral system, it helps you move beyond temptation and instills new belief patterns around finances. It does require a commitment from you to follow the system as it was designed. If you've drawn your line in the sand already and have fully committed to uncovering your own financial truth, stay focused and temptation will no longer be your enemy.

The Profit First system is designed to squash the temptation to borrow from the **Profit** or **Tax** accounts, but if you know you would be tempted to use the money in these accounts when or if the **Operating Expenses** run low, listen up: ***You will need to open two extra accounts at a second bank across town where it will be harder to access the money.*** These are called the No-temptation accounts!

In addition to the five accounts at the main bank, you'll have two more accounts (in a bank across town) to hold the money in the **Profit** and **Tax** accounts.

Remember, the **Profit** and **Tax** accounts will accumulate money over time and are the most tempting to borrow from when or if your **Operating Expenses** account gets low. Once a week, after you make all the allocations and transfers using the accounts at your main bank, you will then move the money from the main bank **Profit** and **Tax** accounts to the respective accounts at the bank across town. Think of these accounts as "holding" accounts. If you choose to utilize the No-temptation accounts, you'll have a total of seven bank accounts instead of five.

YOU DECIDE FOR YOU

Before you get started with Profit First, and prior to facing any challenges, it's a good idea to decide ahead of time if you need these two additional No-temptation accounts at a different bank. Here's a little quiz to help you determine what's best for you.

NO-TEMPTATION SCORE

On a scale of 1 (least tempting) to 10 (most tempting), rate yourself on the following statements. Be totally honest with yourself. Better yet, ask someone who knows you well to rate you at the same time.

Very low temptation. I'd never use this money for a different purpose.	I'd consider it but would be unlikely to follow through.	I'd give it serious thought and would probably use the money after considering all my options.	High-temptation. Yes, I'd use the money because I need it right now.
1–2	3–5	6–7	8–10

	Score
If I see money sitting in any account and I need it to pay bills, I will likely use it.	
If I have an "off" month and my production and collection are significantly down, I will be okay with using money from my Profit or Tax account to pay my bills.	
A piece of needed equipment goes down and requires repair or a new purchase. I am okay with using the Profit or Tax account money for this purpose.	
I am taking a vacation and need a little extra cash to make it happen. I'm willing to "borrow" from the Profit or Tax account for this purpose.	
I'm adding a new, high-level procedure to my offerings and I need some special equipment to fully implement the protocol. I'm fine with using money from my Profit or Tax account for this purpose.	
Add up your score! Total:	

6

Self-Assessment

6

Are you a DIY'er?

If you are savvy with your money and you want to tackle Profit First for Dentists on your own, this chapter is for you. All the instructions and tables are here for you to complete.

If you get started and find yourself lost, I am here to help! Please reach out via email:

barb@barbstackhouse.com

I would love to hear from you! I am not gonna lie, I'd love to help you by having you be a part of our training and coaching program.

There's no pressure at all to sign up for anything with us. I truly want to help you. I promise to answer your questions to the best of my ability with the information I have. So yes, go ahead and send me an email.

Now, back to those of you who want to complete your own Self-Assessment.

THE PROFIT FIRST FOR DENTISTS SELF-ASSESSMENT

Now that you know the core principles of Profit First, it's time to find out how you too can make it work in your business. Remember, all the money will flow into the **Income** account and then, once a week, you will allocate by percentage to the other four core accounts: **Profit**, **Owner's Compensation**, **Tax**, and **Operating Expenses**. If you are using the No-temptation accounts, you'll then move money from your **Profit** and **Tax** accounts at your primary bank to your **Profit** and **Tax** accounts at your secondary bank.

- But how do you know what percentage you should allocate?
- How will you make sure you have enough in the **Operating Expenses** account to pay all the bills?
- What if your current situation is really out of whack compared to what you should be doing?

These are all great questions! And you may be thinking of more.

I'm going to walk you through the process, along with the steps to do your own assessment of your dental practice business. This is one of those "got to stick with it" activities. If you find it mind-boggling or confusing, you are not alone. This is why some dentists choose to ask for help. Either way is fine because, first and foremost, we want you to be successful. We know that this is the key piece to getting it right and making Profit First work for you.

PREPARING FOR YOUR SELF-ASSESSMENT

Step 1: ***Gather all the data you're going to need to complete this assessment. Here's a checklist for you.***

- ☐ Profit and loss statement for the immediate last calendar year (January–December)
- ☐ Balance sheet for that same time period (as of December 31 of the immediate last calendar year)
- ☐ Tax returns for the same year
- ☐ Payroll reports for the same year
- ☐ Loan statements for the same year
- ☐ Credit card statements for the same year

Step 2: *Time to do some math.*

- Add up all the loan payments made in the calendar year you are using.
  Write the total here: __________________________

Step 3: *Gather your credit card statements.*

- Check to make sure all of the credit card charges were entered (in QuickBooks or some other accounting software) using the correct account.
- Check to make sure the credit cards have been reconciled each month (just like the bank accounts).

Step 4: *Obtain your payroll report.*

- Are you, the owner-dentist, paid via payroll? If yes, separate your payroll from the team payroll.
- Find your net pay for the time period (year). Net pay is what you took home plus any benefits withheld from your check except taxes.
  Write the total here: __________________________
- Find the total taxes withheld from your payroll checks for the time period.
  Write the total here: __________________________
- Find the total company-paid taxes just for your owner-dentist payroll for the time period.
  Write the total here: __________________________

Step 5: *Check all records for owner draws and other tax deposits.*

- Did you take any member draws or distributions from the company during the time period?
  If yes, write the total here: __________________________

- Did you pay any quarterly tax estimates to the government during the time period?
  If yes, write the total here: ______________________
- Did you pay any additional taxes when you filed your return?
  If yes, write the total here: ______________________

By completing this assessment, you are opening yourself to the truth about your finances. This can sometimes be a bit stressful, especially if you know there are problems evidenced by money struggles.

JOURNAL

How are you feeling about this discovery so far?

____
____
____
____
____
____
____
____
____
____
____
____

All we are looking at is how much cash came into your business and how much cash went out, along with where it went and for what purposes. Money in and money out. Super simple!

If you haven't yet gathered the data in Steps 1 through 5 above, stop now and go do that first.

In a few pages you will find a Self-Assessment table you can use to see where you are and what you need to do, but first I will explain how to use it and what everything means. It looks like this:

PROFIT FIRST FOR DENTISTS SELF-ASSESSMENT						
	Actual Dollars	CAPs	PF Dentist TAPs	PF Dentist Dollars	Compare	Fix
Real Revenue	A1	100%	100%	D1	E1	F1
Profit	A2	B2	C2	D2	E2	F2
Owner's Compensation	A3	B3	C3	D3	E3	F3
Tax	A4	B4	C4	D4	E4	F4
Operating Expenses	A5	B5	C5	D5	E5	F5

TERMINOLOGY

The first number you will enter is the **real revenue**. Here's a quick lesson on this number and some of the terms you may run across.

- **Gross Production:** Total production for the time period prior to any adjustments or write-offs.
- **Net Production:** Total production for the time period after all adjustments or write-offs. This the total collectible amount.
- **Gross Collection:** Total collected and deposited for the time period.
- **Net Collection:** Total collected for the time period, less any refunds (collection adjustments). **This number is the true real revenue**.

In the original *Profit First* book, Mike Michalowicz talks about "top line revenue" and "real revenue." In case you've read his book (or not) and are wondering about these terms as they pertain to dentistry, here are some definitions to help you.

Top line revenue is the total revenue or money that came into your business before payments to a subcontractor, or payments for materials that are regularly more than 20% of this total revenue. (Neither of these situations will occur in a dental practice, so you really don't need to worry about top line revenue)

Real revenue is the total revenue or money that came into your business less any refunds you made to a patient or insurance company. It's the total amount collected and deposited to your bank account less any refunds.

Two terms you will see in this assessment are CAPs and TAPs:

- **CAPs:** Current Allocation Percentages. This is where your business is today.
- **TAPs:** Target Allocation Percentages. This is where you want your business to be in the future.

Follow each step in the directions for each cell. Use the blank table below or print one from my website to enter your numbers into the corresponding cells.

SELF-ASSESSMENT HOW-TO

A1: In the Actual Dollars column in cell **A1**, enter your total collections (**real revenue**) for the twelve-month calendar year you are using. This is your total income from your profit and loss report. In dentistry, you will not have any subcontractors or high materials costs, so there is no need to examine the difference between top line revenue and real revenue. Associate doctors and hygienists are an expense in your business no matter how you have set up their pay structure.

A2: Enter the total dollar amount deposited into a business savings account for the purpose of profit for the twelve-month calendar year. This is the cumulative profit you have sitting in the bank, or that you have distributed to yourself as a bonus on top of—but not to supplement—your salary. If you do not have profit sitting in the bank in a savings account, this means you don't really have profit.

A3: Enter the total of your net salary, plus any member draws or distributions you used personally, plus any personal expenses paid by the business for the twelve-month calendar year. This information will be available from Steps 4 and 5 in the "Preparing for Your Self-Assessment" section above. Personal expenses paid by the business will be found on the profit and loss report. The number you enter in this cell is the total benefit you received as the owner of the business and does not include taxes.

A4: Enter the total tax your company paid on your behalf for the twelve-month calendar year. This number includes all taxes withheld from your payroll, all company matching taxes, and all corporate taxes. If your company structure is such that you take draws from the company for your personal income, only report the total amount of taxes the company actually paid on your behalf. If you were scrambling at the end of the year to pay your taxes from your personal income, do not include this amount unless you took an additional draw from the company specifically to pay your personal income tax.

A5: Enter the total expenses your business paid for the twelve-month calendar year you are using. This includes everything you paid out except profit, owner's compensation, and taxes. Your expenses will be listed on your profit and loss report (sometimes called an income statement). Also be sure to add in the total of all loan payments made for the year, since this will not show up on the profit and loss statement. If you see something called amortization or depreciation, do not include these items because they are considered non-cash. Remember, we are using only cash in and cash out.

B2–B5: These cells will show you your Current Allocation Percentages (CAPs). Even though you haven't been allocating money every week just yet, we've now organized your money into these four categories so we can see where you currently stand. It's now time to do the math and calculate the percentages:

Divide **A2** by **A1**. Multiply the answer by 100. Enter the result (as %) in **B2**.
Divide **A3** by **A1**. Multiply the answer by 100. Enter the result (as %) in **B3**.
Divide **A4** by **A1**. Multiply the answer by 100. Enter the result (as %) in **B4**.
Divide **A5** by **A1**. Multiply the answer by 100. Enter the result (as %) in **B5**.

C2–C5: Enter the Profit First for Dentists percentages in the Target Allocation Percentages (TAPs) column. Use the Ranges and Averages table below and enter the percentage in the Average column. These are the average numbers I have compiled since I began implementing Profit First with Dentists across the United States. It is worthwhile to note that I work with single owner-dentists or two-dentist partnerships with one or two locations only. These percentages may not be reflective of large group practices. I also included the range for each category so you can see that there are wide differences between practices. This is due to many factors, the most prominent being the level of Preferred Provider Organization (PPO) involvement, the number of employees in the practice, debt load, and the skill level of the dentist.

Your target could be anywhere in the Range column numbers. Refer to your CAPs to determine where you are now. Then think about where you want to go. How much and by what percentage do you want to change?

U.S. DENTAL PRACTICE RANGES & AVERAGES

Real Revenue Range of $3M and Under	Range	Average %
Real Revenue	100%	100%
Profit	1-20%	6%
Owner's Compensation	12-25%	17%
Tax	7-15%	10%
Operating Expenses	55-75%	67%

QUESTION:

How much and by what percentage do you want to change? ______________________

Remember, this is not where you start but where you want to end up. It's also important to be realistic, because unrealistic goals kill motivation. The average is provided for information and as a guide. It is not there as a tool for you to judge yourself. We all start somewhere. The point is that we start!

If you have already busted through the average given here, good for you! What's your next level? Don't let my findings of averages hold you back. I believe that every dental practice owner who believes they can do better will benefit from the Profit First model. If you are satisfied with your profit and believe your business is as profitable as possible already, then don't do anything different. Keep doing what you're doing. But if you're like all the other dentists I speak with who know they can do better, who feel the struggle every day, then this model is for you. I know it works for dentists because I see it working for my clients as I guide them through the setup and implementation process.

D1–D5: We'll complete some more math equations for this row. Have your calculator ready. Using the TAPs column percentages, we'll figure out the dollar amount for each category using your current real revenue.

D1 = Your real revenue.

For now, use the same number you entered in **A1**. Simply copy the number from **A1** to **D1**.

Next, multiply the real revenue number in **D1** by the TAP for each row and write down this number in dollars.

D1 multiplied by **C2** = **D2**.

Enter as a total dollar amount for each item in this row.

D1 multiplied by **C3** = **D3**

D1 multiplied by **C4** = **D4**

D1 multiplied by **C5** = **D5**

These are your target Profit First for Dentists dollar amounts. Sometimes this is painful or stressful to see. Welcome to the wake-up call! I hope these numbers get you a little bit excited for change.

Remember, you are using an average percentage. You may need to adjust your own TAPs depending on where you fall in the ranges given. You may also want to try using a higher real revenue number based on the projected growth percentage you anticipate for the coming year.

E1–E5: Column **E** is the **COMPARE** column. This shows the difference between the current dollar amount and the target dollar amount. Take your actual dollar amount in column **A** and subtract your target amount in column **D**. You'll likely have some negative numbers. Write down the numbers in column **E**. A negative number means this category is experiencing a loss that you'll need to make up. For example, if you've never had a **Profit** account or saved money in a business account before, you'll see a negative number in Profit. This is the amount you'll need to make up for this account. Most likely, not all accounts will show a negative number. It's typical for the **Operating Expenses** account to have a positive number. This represents the excess being spent in this category. The comparison number will show you how much you need to cut from this category.

Here are the formulas to do the math:
A1 minus **D1** = **E1**
A2 minus **D2** = **E2**
A3 minus **D3** = **E3**
A4 minus **D4** = **E4**
A5 minus **D5** = **E5**

F1–F5: This is the **FIX** column, and you will write in the word INCREASE or DECREASE based on which direction the dollar amount needs to adjust.

For example, if your Profit in **A1** is $0 and your Profit in **D1** is $20,000, your comparison is a negative $20,000 and needs to INCREASE. Write the word INCREASE in the **F** column in the Profit row. If the number in the COMPARE column is a positive number, you'll use the word DECREASE in the **F** column.

Below is an example of a completed Self-Assessment.

SAMPLE COMPLETED SELF-ASSESSMENT

	Actual Dollars	CAPs	PF Dentist %	PF Dentist Dollars	Compare	Fix
Real Revenue	A1 $1,200,000	B1 100%	C1 100%	D1 $1,200,000	E1 $0	F1 None
Profit	A2 $0	B2 0%	C2 6%	D2 $72,000	E2 ($72,000)	F2 Increase
Owner's Compensation	A3 $192,000	B3 16%	C3 17%	D3 $204,000	E3 ($12,000)	F3 Increase
Tax	A4 $84,000	B4 7%	C4 10%	D4 $120,000	E4 ($36,000)	F4 Increase
Operating Expenses	A5 $924,000	B5 77%	C5 67%	D5 $804,000	E5 $120,000	F5 Decrease

These numbers are quite typical of many dental practices. The high overhead, or operating expense, is keeping this dentist from realizing the true benefits of practice ownership. It's obvious what needs to happen in this business. Operating expenses must be scrutinized for any over-expenditure, and that money directed to the other three accounts. Remember, this will happen over time with a plan in place.

This assessment brings instant clarity to the business owner and can feel embarrassing at first. Embarrassment leads to hiding. Hiding the problem is what got the dentist to this point. It's now time to embrace the clarity and start taking the steps needed to improve the health of the business.

It's time to stop thinking that more production will solve the problem. Profit is not an event. It's a habit, built week by week over time. Slow and steady wins the race.

IT'S YOUR TURN: ACTION TIME!

You have gathered your data and read the instructions, so now it's time to complete your own assessment. You need to do this if you want to move forward with Profit First in your business.

Use the Profit First for Dentists Self-Assessment table on the next page or go to **www.profitfirstdentist.com** and download a blank copy of it from the Resources tab.

Do not let embarrassment or procrastination get in the way of this step! Get serious. Get with it. Get going!

PROFIT FIRST FOR DENTISTS SELF-ASSESSMENT

	Actual Dollars	CAPs	PF Dentist TAPs	PF Dentist Dollars	Compare	Fix
Real Revenue	A1	100%	100%	D1	E1	F1
Profit	A2	B2	C2	D2	E2	F2
Owner's Compensation	A3	B3	C3	D3	E3	F3
Tax	A4	B4	C4	D4	E4	F4
Operating Expenses	A5	B5	C5	D5	E5	F5

JOURNAL

Now that you've completed the Self-Assessment, reflect for a moment on your next step to implement Profit First in your business. What is that step for you and how will you accomplish it?

7

Making It All Work

7

Dental/Dental Hygiene School required a lot of time studying and learning. None of us went from A to Z overnight (or at least, I didn't). There were challenges. There were failures. There were celebrations. We were molded and shaped into the professionals we are today. Our beliefs were challenged. We learned new concepts. We learned to question things. We learned to get to the root cause of problems.

It's no different with Profit First and your money. Give yourself some grace when you first start out. There's no quiz or exam to pass. This is not a go big or go home kind of proposition. In fact, trying to do too much all at once will put your finances over the edge and likely you'll quit and go back to your old way of doing things. And how's that working for you?

QUESTIONS

What have you tried in the past to help you understand your finances better?

Did you stick with it?

YES NO

Are you still using it today?

YES NO

Have you tried using the Profit First System before?

YES NO

If you answered yes to the last question, what were the challenges? What part(s) of the system, if any, are you still using?

I trust you've read this far because you're serious about Profit First and you want to make sure you do it correctly for a dental practice. I want you to be successful. This method is powerful, and it works!

CAPS TO TAPS

Just like dentistry, Profit First has its own jargon. These acronyms are important to understand.

- **CAPs**: Current allocation percentages. This is where your business is today.
- **TAPs**: Target allocation percentages. This is where you want your business to be in the future.

In Chapter Six, you completed your own assessment (hopefully you have this done). If you didn't do this step or you're stuck trying to do it and need help, please reach out. Send a message to **Barb@BarbStackhouse.com**.

Once you have your own assessment completed, with your CAPs and TAPs, you'll need to create a plan for how you'll implement the changes over time. Remember, we didn't start seeing patients on the first day of dental school. Likewise, you're not going to start with the TAPs. However, you do have to start somewhere.

Perhaps your CAP for Profit has been 0% in the past. You may decide your TAP for Profit is 10%, but you don't start out next week using the 10% allocation for Profit. That's a recipe for disaster and you'll end up robbing the **Profit** account to pay the bills. Then you will feel like a failure and quit. Please don't do this!

The best way to move from point A to point B in the Profit First model is to start with baby steps and go slow. If you need two or three quarters to make the first changes, so be it. No one is going to judge you—except maybe yourself. And that is just chatter in your head. The committee up there doesn't know what it's talking about. Seriously, though, any movement you make in the right direction to make your business more profitable is a win. You must stick with the plan.

JOURNAL

It's time now to get real with the numbers in your practice's finances. You've already faced your CAPs. This means you are face to face with your own financial reality. How does it feel?

If your percentages are close to or less than the averages I shared in Chapter Six, you may be feeling pretty good at this point. But if your percentages are woefully over the averages, you might be stressing a bit.

At first, you may think there's no way you can do this. Remember the committee that chatters in your head? Remember all the stories from Chapter One that we tell ourselves? They're all just made-up stories. Every time you feel the stress coming on: remember, **they are all just made-up stories**. Yes, they feel real and raw right now, but until you change the story in your head, you'll keep on believing it. And that is what got you to where you are now.

Ask yourself: Could you change things by just a few percentage points in each category? Why, yes, of course you can. That's your starting point. Here is a chart where you can plot out your plan.

MY PLAN FOR CHANGE					
Category	Current %	QTR 1 Target%	QTR 2 Target%	QTR 3 Target%	QTR 4 Target%
Real Revenue					
Profit					
Owner's Compensation					
Tax					
Operating Expenses					

TRIM THE OVERHEAD

There are 3 ways to improve profitability in your business.

1. Produce More
2. Reduce Expenses
3. Do a combination of both

It's important to pay attention to the cost of doing business. Expenses can creep up if you're not paying attention.

We're going to divide the overhead, or operating expenses, into two main categories. They are "fixed expenses" and "variable expenses." There will be subcategories within these two main categories, but we'll keep it all super simple here. Once you break down the expenses into the fixed or variable categories, it's much easier to see where you can start reducing expenses.

A fixed expense is one that typically remains at the same, or nearly the same, dollar amount every month. When the monthly collection increases, the fixed expense percentage goes down. When the monthly collection decreases, the fixed expense percentage goes up.

A variable expense is one that typically fluctuates or changes right along with the changes in collection from month to month. It is likely that the percentage for variable expenses will remain consistent. And it makes sense that if you produce and collect more, your supply and lab costs will also increase. There will also be other expenses, like merchant fees, that go up as well. You may well spend more on marketing, too.

Fixed expenses include the following operating expenses:

- Team compensation
- Occupancy
- Equipment and debt payments

Variable expenses include the following operating expenses:

- Dental supplies
- Lab
- Marketing
- Business administration and other

As a general rule for a dental practice, the fixed expenses should not exceed 40%. Ideally, you want them to be about 35%

of revenue if possible. If the percentage is way over in this category, start by looking at revenue.

QUESTIONS

What is your current monthly Fixed Expense Dollar Amount? (Remember to include all loan payments—they are usually fixed amounts.) ____________________

What % of your average monthly revenue is this? ____________________

Ask yourself:

- Is the schedule fully booked?
- Does the day fall apart at the last minute?
- Do I have enough active patients to support the amount of time available?

If you are unable to make changes to increase revenue in a timely manner, you may need to look at ways to reduce your fixed expenses. It's a bit more of a challenge, but it can be done.

As for variable expenses, the general rule is not to exceed 30% and ideally keep it to 25% of revenue or less.

QUESTIONS

What is your current monthly Variable Expense Dollar Amount? ____________________

What % of your monthly revenue is this? ____________________

Scrutinize every expense and ask yourself these questions:

- Is this expense necessary to deliver quality dentistry?
- Does this expense benefit our patients and our team?
- Does this expense directly contribute to our services?
- Is this expense necessary to keep the doors open?

I think you get the idea here. Nothing is sacred. Question every expense and reduce it where possible or eliminate it altogether.

Keep in mind that these suggested percentages include all cash that went out of the office to pay any expense or loan payment in any given month. You will not find these totals or percentages on your profit and loss report. And this is why it always seems like something is missing from that report—because it is!

What I'm sharing is a very simple description, and there is certainly more to a practice or business financial picture than this. However, I've provided a great, simple foundation to operate from. The **Operating Expenses** account will be used to pay all of these fixed and variable expenses. If you are overspending somewhere, the account will be screaming at you with low funds available.

WEEKLY RHYTHM

With Profit First for Dentists, we've found that a weekly rhythm works best. There are a lot of moving parts in a dental practice, and things can change quickly, so having weekly allocations seem to work much better.

Every day, the practice collections are deposited in the **Income** account. These deposits sit in this account and accumulate until the end of the week.

Once the week is closed out and the money has hit the bank, figure out the allocation amount based on the percentage you determined and then open your online banking and make the transfers.

QUESTION

What day of the week will you determine your allocations and make your transfers? ____________________

ACTION STEP

Now put a reminder on your calendar that repeats every week.

QUARTERLY CELEBRATION!

At the end of each quarter, it's celebration time! This is when you take your profit distribution. Remember, it's your reward for taking the risk to be a business owner. It's your pay for all the other business things you do. Calculate your profit distribution at 50%

of the total deposits into the **Profit** account for the quarter. Leave the remainder in the account to build up and provide you with a "rainy day" fund. When cash reserves build up over time in this account, you will find a certain relief of stress and peace of mind.

> **ACTION STEP**
> ***Put a reminder on your calendar for your Quarterly Profit Distributions on April 1, July 1, October 1, and January 1.***

GETTING STARTED: A TO-DO LIST

Have you contacted your bookkeeper and/or CPA to let them know what you are doing?

YES NO

If so, how did that meeting go?

____

____

____

____

Do you feel confident your bookkeeper/CPA will support you in doing Profit First?

YES NO

Have you set up your bank accounts?

YES NO

Did you complete the Self-Assessment?

YES NO

Do you have your CAPs and TAPs and a plan in place to reach them?

YES NO

What will you do to cut expenses?

What will you do to increase revenue?

8

Manage Debt and Plan for the Future

8

PERSONAL AND BUSINESS DEBT

It's good to understand both personal and business debt. They both impact the practice. Your personal lifestyle affects what you do in the practice and how the business will support you. It's critical to make good decisions both personally and professionally when it comes to debt. If you have multiple loans for different things, it's a good idea to first take stock of the situation. Make a list of all your personal debt and all business debt. Here's a sample list to get you started. You will need to include the amount of debt for each category and then add up these numbers for a total.

ACTION STEP

On the next pages, write down the total amount you owe and the monthly payment for debts in each of the following categories.

PERSONAL DEBT

	Total Owed	Payment
School Debt		
Home Loan		
Automobile Loans		
Second Home Loan		
Credit Card Debt (not paid off every month)		
Family Loan		
Other Personal Debt		

BUSINESS DEBT

	Total Owed	Payment
Practice build-out and/or practice purchase loan(s)		
Equipment loan(s)		
Line of Credit		
Credit Card Debt (not paid off every month)		
Family Loan		
Mortgage on Facility (you own your own building)		
Other Business Debt		

GETTING OUT OF DEBT

Once you clearly understand your debt, you might be wondering how you can pay it off sooner rather than later. I'm all for paying off debt, but not at the expense of a **Profit** account. I've watched dentists plow all their extra cash into debt payoff only to find themselves in a low-production month six months down the road and borrowing more money to pay the bills. And yes, they borrow with credit cards. So, they end up in a cycle that just never seems to end.

With any plan to pay down debt, there must also be a plan to set aside profit first. In fact, the Profit First system works great for decreasing debt load. More on that in just a minute.

First, you must put a freeze on debt! **No more DEBT!** You must not acquire any new loans, no matter what. This is a commitment you make to yourself and your business. It seems so simple, but sticking to it can be difficult. If your go-to plan when you need to get out of a pinch with your finances is to get a loan or use a credit card, this step may be harder for you. You owe it to yourself to do this.

You must shift your thinking to a mindset of saving money, no matter what. Saving money means cash in the bank. It's been proven that a slow, methodical practice of saving a little bit each week works. You build the habit of saving. Setting aside your profit first easily creates this habit. Even though you have debt, you still need to save money. The point is, you build a new habit and strengthen your resolve with the debt freeze.

Once your **Profit** account has built up over a quarter time period, you'll calculate your profit distribution. As the owner, you will typically take 50% of the profit deposits as a distribution; however, if you are actively working to pay down debt, this percentage may change. You may choose to take a smaller profit distribution for yourself and opt to use a larger percentage to make a payment on the principal of a loan you are working to pay off. For example, you might decide to use 70 or 80% of the total of the profit deposits for a distribution and keep 10% for yourself, using the remainder to pay down debt.

ACTION STEP

Use the snowball system to pay down debt.

Step 1: List your debts from smallest to largest regardless of interest rate.
Step 2: Make minimum payments on all your debts except the smallest.
Step 3: Pay as much as possible on your smallest debt.
Step 4: Repeat until each debt is paid in full.

If you find that your biggest issue is credit card debt, start paying on the card with the least total balance. Pay it off and then work on the next credit card. It's like the snowball system but instead you are focusing on the debt with the highest interest rate.

Never forget this: CASH in the bank = POWER to make better money decisions.

FUTURE GROWTH IN YOUR PRACTICE

You may be wondering how you will grow your practice if your focus is funding the **Profit** account and getting out of debt.

JOURNAL

First, let's define "practice growth." What does it mean to you, the owner of the practice?

There are many numbers that may be measured and attributed to business growth in a dental practice. Here's a list to get started.

- Increased production
- Increased number of active patients
- Increased collection
- Increased number of team members or providers
- Increased number of locations

JOURNAL

What does business growth look like for you?

What is your vision for your business?

How does this vision reflect your business goals for growth?

9

Tax Strategies for Dentists Part A: United States Part B: Canada

9

PART A: UNITED STATES

Contributed by Drew Hinrichs; Engage Advisors
(from *Profit First for Dentists*)

Tax strategies are an important part of owning a business. Finding your own level of risk with perfectly legal tax mitigation efforts is the first important step to take.

Some CPAs are willing to be more aggressive than others when it comes to filing taxes and utilizing creative ways to reduce income taxes. There is always the risk of a red flag with the IRS that could lead to an audit. This is where you need to decide how comfortable you are with this approach.

QUESTION

When you think about your CPA utilizing strategies to mitigate income tax, rate the level of risk you are comfortable with on a scale of 1 to 10, with 1 being very low risk and 10 being very high risk (you want to use every strategy out there). (Circle one)

1 2 3 4 5 6 7 8 9 10

JOURNAL

Why did you choose that number?
Explain how you arrived at it.

QUESTIONS

Do you work with a CPA who shares
your level of risk tolerance?

YES NO

Do you know the level of risk tolerance your CPA has?

YES NO

Have you ever had a conversation with your CPA about this?

YES NO

It is important to work with a CPA who is like-minded with you on the strategies you are willing to use and the risk level you are willing to tolerate. I might add, this is also important to consider with any financial advisor you employ.

YOUR LEGAL BUSINESS ENTITY

Depending on the type of legal entity you have will impact your tax liability and the percentage you will allocate and transfer to the **Tax** account. This is not a one size fits all for dental practices.

Sole Proprietor

This is the simplest, cheapest, and fastest way out there to do business. You do business as you. The business is your name. You are the business.

One issue with this type of entity is the lack of legal protection for your business. Yes, insurance protects you but a legal entity like a corporation can also protect you personally.

Typically, a sole proprietor will pay estimated income tax quarterly. Your CPA will help you determine how much you should send to the government each quarter.

Limited Liability Company

This is the entity that is most common for dental practices to do business. It is also a very simple way to conduct business. The primary difference is the business is no longer synonymous with you personally. It's now a separate legal entity formed under the rules and regulations of the State where you are located.

This arrangement does provide some basic legal protection for your personal assets. It also allows you to grow as a business and still work for you. With an LLC (Limited Liability Company), you can choose how you want to file your tax returns, either as a sole proprietor or an S corporation. Your CPA and attorney can help you with this decision and what will be best for you should you choose the LLC entity.

C Corporation

This is the least common way for a dental practice to do business. The C corporation is a business registered and filed with the Secretary of State in your state where you do business.

The big difference is that now the corporation files its own tax return, however the profits from the business do not flow through to the owner's personal tax return. Instead, the corporation profits are taxed, and those earnings are retained in the business. If the owner wants to disperse any earnings, they must take a dividend on which they will be taxed as personal income. This leads to a double taxation.

There may be other reasons for utilizing a C Corporation entity and if this is your set up, it would be a good idea to have a conversation regarding this with your business attorney and CPA. I recommend consulting with a Dental Specific CPA to learn more.

S Corporation

This is an election that is filed with the IRS once your business chooses to be incorporated. The tax advantages include the profits of the business passing through to the shareholder. This entity also requires the shareholder to be on payroll with a reasonable compensation.

QUESTIONS

Of these 4, what is your legal entity? ____________________

Are you satisfied with this legal entity? Or are you thinking there could be a better option for your business? Explain.

If you are unsure about your type of business entity or have questions about this, please seek the advice of your CPA. I would recommend a dental specific CPA who has experience, and you are confident can guide you.

TAX DEDUCTIONS

The risk level you identified at the beginning of this chapter will help you determine what tax deductions you are willing to take and which ones you are averse to. You need to find your own comfort level.

Do always report all income to the IRS and to your CPA. Hiding money is never a good idea.

Do take the deductions that are possible. This will help you reduce your taxes substantially. Again, you will need to find your own comfort level with these deductions.

Here are some possible deductions that I recommend you speak with your accountant about.

- **Automobile Deductions:** This is a deduction that can be tricky so it's best to talk with your CPA to see if you have a vehicle that qualifies. You may also consider taking a mileage deduction for the use of your personal vehicle when doing work for your business. Again, the tax codes change from year to year so be sure to discuss this with a professional.
- **Hiring Your Children:** If you have children, this is an option as a deduction for the business and a way for your kids to earn tax free money. The limit changes, so check each year to see how much they may earn tax free. They can do jobs such as cleaning, helping with social media, or even modeling for social media posts. You may also take advantage of a Roth IRA contribution or fund your children's education as part of a plan for tax mitigation.
- **Write Off Your Travel:** When traveling for continuing education, the expenses are deductible. When you tack on vacation time on either end of the CE trip, it's easy to make vacation expenses deductible. Other ways to expense travel include hosting a "board of directors" meeting or possibly checking out a new lab or supplier.
- **Home Office:** It is possible to conduct business from a Home Office by doing things like checking on patients, bookkeeping, online banking, or logging into the office and doing notes, etc. The home office must be a dedicated

office space and used for work. Again, speak with your CPA about this option.

- **Rent Your Home for a Business Meeting:** You could host a team meeting or retreat at your home or have a "board of directors" meeting and have your business pay you a rental fee. There are some stipulations on making this work, so you need to know ahead of time what the tax code says.

JOURNAL

What deductions are you currently taking advantage of?

Are there other deductions you would like to consider?

____

____

____

____

____

____

If you haven't already, when will you discuss these options with your CPA?

____

TAX-SAVING INVESTMENTS

- **Retirement Plan Contributions:** It's best to find a good financial planner to help you making these important decisions. Choose a fiduciary planner to help you. You'll also want to include a tax strategist in your discussions. Making regular contributions to a retirement plan is one way to offset current income tax. Be aware though that when you use the money (during retirement), you will pay the income tax then.
- **Tax Savings Investments:** By saving money on taxes and working to reduce your overhead, you'll have additional cash available. Use this cash to invest for the future in ways that will make more money. This may be through investments that utilize compounded interest or savings or investment plans.
- **Other Investment Strategies:** This category includes real estate or other business investments. It's important to know what you are doing, so if you are new to this, hire a professional to help.

JOURNAL

What does your retirement plan look like?

QUESTION

Are you on track to fully fund your plans for the future?

YES NO

If not, how much do you need to save each month to get back on track?

Do you have a financial planner, CPA, and other professionals to help you?

YES NO

If not, what are you doing to find them?

PART B: CANADA

Contributed by April Stroink, BComm; Money Coach

As a Canadian dentist, your journey to building a thriving practice is often accompanied by unique financial complexities and tax considerations. Whether you're newly graduated and starting your own clinic, an associate working in an established practice, or a seasoned practitioner preparing for retirement, understanding how to effectively manage your taxes is a critical part of maximizing your income and safeguarding your wealth.

Tax planning is not just about reducing your tax liability; it's about understanding the broader financial picture, ensuring compliance with Canada's tax laws, and setting up your practice and personal finances in a way that fosters long-term growth.

JOURNAL

What are the current financial and tax-related challenges you face in your dental practice, and how do you think a better understanding of tax planning could help you address them?

Looking ahead, how do you envision tax planning playing a role in achieving your long-term financial goals as a dentist?

OPTIMIZE YOUR INCOME: TAKE ADVANTAGE OF TAX DEDUCTIONS, CREDITS, AND DEFERRALS.

As a dentist in Canada, understanding how to optimize your income through effective tax strategies can make a significant difference in your overall financial health. One of the key components of this process is learning to leverage the tax deductions, credits, and deferrals that are available to you. These strategies help you reduce your taxable income, allowing you to keep more of your earnings, reinvest in your practice, and plan for your financial future.

Let's explore how each of these tools—deductions, credits, and deferrals—can help you retain more of your hard-earned money.

1. MAXIMIZE TAX DEDUCTIONS: REDUCING YOUR TAXABLE INCOME

Tax deductions reduce the amount of income on which you have to pay taxes. As a dentist, there are numerous business and personal expenses that may qualify as tax deductions. Knowing what you can deduct and maintaining proper records is crucial for minimizing your taxable income.

Common Deductions for Canadian Dentists

Practice-Related Expenses: You can deduct a wide variety of expenses that are directly related to running your practice, including:

- **Office rent or mortgage interest:** If you rent or own the property where your practice operates, these costs are deductible.
- **Staff salaries and benefits:** Wages and benefits for employees such as hygienists, administrative staff, and assistants are deductible business expenses.
- **Equipment and supplies:** Purchases of dental equipment, instruments, office supplies, and other materials necessary for your practice can be deducted.

- **Utilities and maintenance costs:** Water, electricity, internet, cleaning services, and other utility bills are eligible expenses
- **Professional dues and subscriptions:** Membership fees for professional associations (e.g., Canadian Dental Association), subscriptions to industry journals, and other similar expenses are deductible.
- **Continuing education and training:** Courses, seminars, and certifications that contribute to your professional development can be deducted as long as they are directly related to your practice.
- **Vehicle and Travel Expenses:** If you use a vehicle for business purposes, such as traveling between multiple clinic locations or attending conferences, a portion of your vehicle-related expenses (fuel, insurance, maintenance) can be deducted. Additionally, business-related travel expenses such as accommodations and meals for conferences or meetings are eligible deductions.
- **Home Office Deduction:** If part of your home is used exclusively for administrative work or managing your practice, you may be able to deduct a portion of home-related expenses (utilities, property taxes, home insurance) related to that space.
- **Depreciation (Capital Cost Allowance - CCA):** For significant purchases such as dental chairs, X-ray machines, or computer systems, you can claim depreciation over several years using the Capital Cost Allowance (CCA). This allows you to deduct a portion of the asset's cost each year, reducing your taxable income.

By claiming all eligible deductions, you reduce your total taxable income, ultimately lowering the amount of tax you owe.

QUESTIONS

Are you aware of all the tax deductions available to you as a Canadian dentist?

YES NO

Have you been taking advantage of these deductions?

YES NO

Has your CPA made you aware of these deductions?

YES NO

2. UTILIZE TAX CREDITS: DIRECTLY REDUCE THE AMOUNT OF TAX YOU PAY

Tax credits directly reduce the amount of taxes you owe and can significantly lower your tax liability. Unlike deductions, which reduce your taxable income, credits reduce your final tax bill dollar-for-dollar.

Common Tax Credits for Dentists

- **Medical Expense Tax Credit (METC):** Dentists may be eligible for the METC for certain medical expenses that are not covered by insurance, especially if they or their family members incur significant medical costs throughout the year.
- **Tuition and Education Credits:** If you or your dependents are still completing dental training or taking eligible courses related to your profession, tuition fees can be claimed as a tax credit.

- **Disability Tax Credit (DTC):**If you or a dependent has a qualifying disability, the DTC can provide substantial tax relief. This is especially relevant for dentists who may have family members with disabilities.
- **Charitable Donations:** If you make charitable donations, including donating to causes related to healthcare or education, you can claim a non-refundable tax credit for eligible donations.
- **Provincial and Territorial Credits:** In addition to federal tax credits, there may be credits available specific to your province or territory. For example, some provinces offer credits for investing in small businesses or making eco-friendly upgrades to your practice.

QUESTIONS

Are you aware of all the tax credits available to you as a Canadian dentist?

YES NO

Have you been taking advantage of these credits?

YES NO

Has your CPA made you aware of these credits?

YES NO

---

3. LEVERAGE TAX DEFERRALS: POSTPONE YOUR TAX LIABILITY

Tax deferrals allow you to postpone paying taxes to a future date, which can be particularly useful if you expect to be in a lower tax bracket later in life, such as during retirement. By deferring taxes, you can take advantage of compounding growth on untaxed amounts, boosting your long-term wealth.

Common Tax Deferral Strategies for Dentists

- **Registered Retirement Savings Plan (RRSP):** Contributions to an RRSP are tax-deductible, meaning they reduce your taxable income in the year they are made. The income generated in the RRSP is tax-deferred, and you won't pay tax on these amounts until you withdraw them during retirement—when you'll likely be in a lower tax bracket.
- **Incorporation and Professional Corporations (PCs):** Many dentists choose to incorporate their practices, allowing them to retain profits in the corporation and defer personal taxes on that income. By leaving excess funds in the corporation, rather than drawing them as salary or dividends, you can take advantage of lower corporate tax rates and defer personal tax until the money is withdrawn at a later time. This is particularly advantageous for dentists with a high income who do not need to withdraw all of their earnings immediately.
- **Tax-Free Savings Account (TFSA):** While contributions to a TFSA are not tax-deductible, all growth in the account (interest, dividends, and capital gains) is tax-free. Withdrawals from a TFSA are also not taxable, making it an excellent tool for tax-free growth and future spending.

- **Income Splitting:** Dentists who are incorporated may be able to split income with family members (spouses or children) who are in lower tax brackets, which reduces the overall family tax burden. This strategy can be implemented through the payment of dividends or salaries to family members who provide legitimate services to the practice.

QUESTIONS

Are you aware of all the tax deferral strategies available to you as a Canadian dentist?

YES NO

Have you been taking advantage of these strategies?

YES NO

Has your CPA made you aware of these strategies?

YES NO

MAKE TAX OPTIMIZATION WORK FOR YOU

By understanding and applying these tax deductions, credits, and deferrals, you can significantly reduce your tax burden and retain more of your hard-earned money. The key is to develop a proactive tax plan tailored to your specific situation as a dentist, one that adapts to your personal and professional goals.

A comprehensive tax strategy will not only improve your cash flow in the short term but also ensure that you are well-positioned for long-term financial success. Whether you're reinvesting in your practice, saving for retirement, or planning for major life events, optimizing your tax situation is a fundamental step toward financial freedom.

JOURNAL

What specific tax deductions, credits, or deferrals are you currently using in your practice, and how might optimizing these strategies help you increase cash flow and move closer to financial freedom?

As you plan for retirement, how can a proactive tax strategy help you achieve financial independence and secure the lifestyle you envision for your post-career years?*

WHY TAX PLANNING MATTERS FOR DENTISTS

The Canadian tax system offers numerous opportunities for dental professionals to save money, but it also presents unique challenges. With the right knowledge and planning, you can navigate these complexities, allowing you to focus on what matters most—providing excellent care for your patients and building a prosperous future for yourself.

By taking control of your tax strategy, you can ensure that your practice thrives financially, not just today but for years to come.

DISCLAIMER: THE IMPORTANCE OF WORKING WITH A TAX PROFESSIONAL SPECIALIZING IN CANADIAN DENTISTRY

The tax information and strategies provided in this workbook are intended for general guidance and educational purposes only. While we have made every effort to ensure accuracy, tax laws and regulations are complex and constantly evolving. As a dentist, your financial and tax situation may involve unique factors that require specialized attention.

We strongly recommend working with a qualified tax professional who has experience in Canadian dental practices. A tax expert familiar with the intricacies of dental practice finances and relevant Canadian tax regulations will be able to offer personalized advice, help you maximize deductions and credits, and ensure compliance with both federal and provincial tax laws.

This guidebook should not be relied upon as a substitute for professional tax advice. Each individual's financial situation is different, and applying general tax strategies without proper guidance may result in missed opportunities or unintended consequences.

Consulting with a tax professional who understands your specific needs as a Canadian dentist will provide you with tailored strategies that can help you optimize your tax planning and achieve your financial goals effectively and safely.

10

Facing the Challenges

10

QUESTION

Be honest here, are you thinking this is all just too much, and that you can do it by yourself with a spreadsheet?

YES NO

If you answered yes, you are not alone. Our brains are always looking for ways to simplify anything we do, and this is no different. We talk ourselves into thinking it's just the theory that matters and we really don't need to open all those bank accounts.

I'm here to tell you this way of thinking is a big fat lie! Theory is one thing, behavior is another.

As with anything we expect to accomplish, action must be taken. It is this repeated behavior that makes Profit First different. It's the design of the system using natural human behaviors around money that makes it successful.

It is simple. It is behaviorally sound.

QUESTION

Have you found yourself getting caught up in the details, making sure everything is exact before you can get started with allocations and transfers?

YES NO

It's common for dentists to be analytical. It's the way dental school trains them to be. So, it makes sense that this analytical, check and re-check mindset spills over into other areas of the business.

If you find yourself in this cycle, take heart, you are not alone.

Know this, Profit First does not have to be perfect to get started. And if numbers are not your thing or they scare you, reach out to me! I'm here to help.

QUESTION

Have you found yourself so excited about Profit First that you want to jump in head-first, believing that your business can sustain putting 20% in the Profit account from the start?

YES NO

Jumping ahead is a mistake. It's important to follow each step in the process. Have a plan to start small and gradually work your way up to the best percentages for your business. The target goals must be realistic for this system to work.

Do not give up because of Too Much Too Fast! Again, reach out for some help. You don't have to go it alone.

QUESTION

Are you secretly starting this process on your own, thinking that you can do it by yourself and that if you fail, no one will know?

YES NO

Having an accountability partner is one of the best ways to stay on track. Your commitment will stay stronger when someone else is there to cheer you on and check in with you.

You can tip toe around and try to make it work, or you can tell someone and ask for assistance. It's your choice.

Having a coach or accountability partner is one of the best ways to ensure success. Finding an experienced coach in the method you are trying to achieve is also important. Look for the best! You deserve it.

QUESTION

Who is your accountability partner? ______________________

Would you like to have a trained Profit First coach?

YES NO

JOURNAL

Describe in detail the steps you have you taken toward setting your business up to run as a Profit First company. Or, if you haven't yet acted, what is your plan?

One of the big hurdles to overcome is the one that makes up stuff between your ears. Yes, our own minds can convince us that something is true, when in reality, we've never tested it.

If you believe you must choose between "business growth" and "profit," your mind is telling you a lie.

Growth and profit go hand in hand. When you build a profitable business, you will have the resources for expansion and growth…if that is your desire.

If cash flow is a problem, there are basically 3 things you can do to improve the situation.

They are:

1. Reduce Expenses
2. Increase Revenue
3. A combination of both

It's time to go searching for the hidden profit in your business.

AFTER REVIEWING YOUR EXPENSES

What expenses/overhead will you cut? Make a list:

What are the necessary expenses/overhead that you'll keep? Make a List:

Are there any expenses/overhead you can re-negotiate or change to reduce the cost? Make a list:

It's so very important to answer these questions! If you don't act now with your expenses, you may end up in a situation where you are tempted to "steal" money from another account to pay the bills. The is a big "red flag!" Listen to what your business is telling you and take the necessary steps to increase profits!

11

What Are You Waiting For?

11

Now is the time for action! Everything we do or create is always created twice. Once in the mind and then again when we actually do it. ***It's time to do it!***

CREATE YOUR OWN PROFIT FIRST LIFESTYLE!
FOLLOW THESE SIMPLE STEPS:

Week One: Notify your accountant of the changes you are making and set up the bank accounts!

Week Two: Make sure all auto pay debits are moved to the **Operating Expenses** account. (This may take a few weeks to accomplish.)

Month One: Make sure you know your percentage allocations and begin making the bank transfers each week. Listen to what your business is telling you via the bank account balances. Adjust if needed. Continue each week and month.

Quarter One: Take your Profit Distribution. The dates for these distributions from the **Profit** account are April 1, July 1, October 1, and January 1 every year.

Year One: Conduct a review of the numbers and the cash flow. Adjust as needed and possible.

JOURNAL

What will your personal spending goals look like?

How much will you take out of the business to support your lifestyle?

How much will you invest in your personal future and eventual exit from your practice and business? What are you waiting for?

____

____

____

____

____

____

____

____

____

____

____

____

____

Send an email to* barb@barbstackhouse.com *and let me know your plan! I'd love to hear from you.

Acknowledgments

After writing the book *Profit First for Dentists* and working with many dentists implementing this model, I found it was time to create a guidebook. Why? So that more dentists could find the help they deserve to get Profit First working in their practice/business.

My goal is to help any dentist entrepreneur be as profitable as possible. Many dentists like you reading this book find they want to try it on their own. I hope this guidebook helps you achieve what you are looking to do.

I also know many of you will want some help. I want to be the one you call on. My clinical background along with my many years of business experience make me qualified for the job!

I am grateful for all the dentists I've helped along the way. I've learned something from each of you. Thank you!

I am equally grateful for the Profit First Professionals organization started by Mike Michalowicz and Ron Saharyan. Without this organization, I wouldn't be where I am today…especially writing this guidebook!

I've been fortunate to have wonderful mentors along my journey in Dental Practice Management. Working alongside Dr. Mike Schuster for many years at The Schuster Center has been a key part of my professional development. I'm very grateful for that opportunity.

Personally, my number one fan is my husband, Kevin. From high school sweethearts to celebrating 45 years of marriage in 2024, he truly is my best friend and biggest cheerleader. I know

I'm lucky, but the truth is we both work on our relationship. It gets better every day. I live a wonderful life on a seven-acre piece of property with a beautiful barn home, a horse named Duke, two goats named Dolly and Reba, and two dogs named Otis and Luci. What more could a girl want?

Thank you for reading *Profit First for Dentists* and this companion *Guidebook!* It is appreciated.

Contact the Author

Email:
barb@barbstackhouse.com

Website:
www.profitfirstdentist.com

Facebook Group for Dentists:
https://group.profitfirstdentist.com

YouTube:
https://youtube.profitfirstdentist.com

LinkedIn:
https://www.linkedin.com/in/barb-stackhouse-2624569/

Instagram:
https://www.instagram.com/profitfirstfordentists/

PROFIT FIRST FOR DENTISTS SOFTWARE

Seven years ago, when I started this company, I knew dentists would need a way to track their data and measure their success with the Profit First model.

Since then, I have given all my clients access to try this software and see for themselves if they want to make it part of their Profit First process. Many have stayed connected and are still using it today.

Profit First for Dentists and this *Guidebook* provide the methods and tools to do your own Profit First Assessment and Roll Out Plan, but I want to make one more tool available to you: the **Profit First for Dentists Software**. In addition, I have created training videos to go with the software and a sample review of a report.

For two months of complimentary access to the software and the training videos, please visit my website and complete the request for access at:

www.profitfirstdentist.com/ freesoftwareaccess

Made in the USA
Monee, IL
13 September 2026

63137528R00083